RELIGIONS: ANCIENT AND MODERN.

Foolscap 8vo. 1s. net per volume.

It is intended in this series to present to a large public the SALIENT FEATURES, first of the GREAT RELIGIONS, secondly of the GREAT PHILOSOPHIES, and thirdly of the GREAT LITERARY and ARTISTIC REPUTATIONS of the Human Race.

PANTHEISM: ITS STORY AND SIGNIFICANCE.
By J. ALLANSON PICTON, M.A. Author of *The Religion of the Universe*, etc.

RELIGION OF ANCIENT GREECE.
By Miss JANE HARRISON, Fellow of Newnham College, Author of *Prolegomena to the Study of Greek Religion*, etc.

ANIMISM.
By EDWARD CLODD, Author of *Pioneers of Evolution*.

RELIGIONS OF ANCIENT CHINA.
By H. A. GILES, M.A., LL.D. (Aberd.), Professor of Chinese at Cambridge University.

The following Volumes are in preparation:

ISLAM. Mr. T. W. ARNOLD, Assistant Librarian, India Office.

BUDDHISM. 2 vols. Prof. RHYS DAVIDS, LL.D.

HINDUISM. Mr. T. W. ARNOLD.

FETISHISM AND MAGIC. Prof. ALFRED C. HADDON, F.R.S.

THE MYTHOLOGY OF ANCIENT BRITAIN. Mr. CHARLES SQUIRE.

CELTIC RELIGION. Prof. ANWYL.

SCANDINAVIAN RELIGION. Mr. W. A. CRAIGIE.

THE RELIGION OF ANCIENT EGYPT. Prof. FLINDERS PETRIE. F.R.S.

THE RELIGION OF BABYLONIA AND ASSYRIA. Dr. THEOPHILUS G. PINCHES.

.6

acc.no: 146348

N STACK

PANTHEISM

Its Story and Significance

BY J. ALLANSON PICTON
AUTHOR OF "THE RELIGION OF THE
UNIVERSE" "THE MYSTERY OF
MATTER" ETC

LONDON
ARCHIBALD CONSTABLE & CO LTD
1905

BUTLER & TANNER,
THE SELWOOD PRINTING WORKS
FROME, AND LONDON.

CONTENTS

CHAP.		PAGE
	Foreword	7
I.	Pre-Christian Pantheism	16
II.	Post-Christian Pantheism	47
III.	Modern Pantheism	56
	Afterword	79

PANTHEISM

FOREWORD.

Pantheism not Sectarian or even Racial. PANTHEISM differs from the systems of belief constituting the main religions of the world in being comparatively free from any limits of period, climate, or race. For while what we roughly call the Egyptian Religion, the Vedic Religion, the Greek Religion, Buddhism, and others of similar fame have been necessarily local and temporary, Pantheism has been, for the most part, a dimly discerned background, an esoteric significance of many or all religions, rather than a " denomination " by itself. The best illustration of this characteristic of Pantheism is the catholicity of its great prophet Spinoza. For he felt so little antagonism to any Christian sect, that he never urged any member of a church to leave it, but rather encouraged his humbler friends, who sought his advice, to make full use of such spiritual privileges as they appreciated most. He could not, indeed, content himself with the fragmentary forms of any sectarian creed. But in the few writings which he made some effort to adapt to the popular understanding, he seems to think it possible that the faith of Pantheism might some day leaven all religions alike. I shall endeavour briefly to sketch the story of that faith, and to suggest its significance for the future. But first we must know what it means.

Meaning of Pantheism. Pantheism, then, being a term derived from two Greek words signifying "all" and "God," suggests to a certain extent its own meaning. Thus, if Atheism be taken to mean a denial of the being of God, Pantheism is its extreme opposite; because Pantheism declares that there is nothing but God. This, however, needs explanation. For no Pantheist has ever held that *everything* is God, any more **God is All.** than a teacher of physiology, in enforcing on his students the unity of the human organism, would insist that every toe and finger is the man. But such a teacher, at least in these days, would almost certainly warn his pupils against the notion that the man can be really

FOREWORD

But not Everything is God.

divided into limbs, or organs, or faculties, or even into soul and body. Indeed, he might without affectation adopt the language of a much controverted creed, so far as to pronounce that "the reasonable soul and flesh is one man"—"one altogether." In this view, the man is the unity of all organs and faculties. But it does not in the least follow that any of these organs or faculties, or even a selection of them, is the man.

Analogy of the Human Organism.

The Analogy Imperfect but Useful.

If I apply this analogy to an explanation of the above definition of Pantheism as the theory that there is nothing but God, it must not be supposed that I regard the parallelism as perfect. In fact, one purpose of the following exposition will be to show why and where all such analogies fail. For Pantheism does not regard man, or any organism, as a true unity. In the view of Pantheism the only real unity is God. But without any inconsistency I may avail myself of common impressions to correct a common mis-impression. Thus, those who hold that the reasonable soul and flesh is one man—one altogether—but at the same time deny that the toe or the finger, or the stomach or

PANTHEISM

the heart, is the man, are bound in consistency to recognise that if Pantheism affirms God to be All in All, it does not follow that Pantheism must hold a man, or a tree, or a tiger to be God.

Excluding, then, such an apparently plausible, but really fallacious inversion of the Pantheistic view of the Universe, I repeat that the latter is **Farther Definition.** the precise opposite of Atheism. So far from tolerating any doubt as to the being of God, it denies that there is anything else. For all objects of sense and thought, including individual consciousness, whether directly observed in ourselves, or inferred as existing in others, are, according to Pantheism, only facets of an infinite Unity, which is "altogether one" in a sense inapplicable to anything else. Because that Unity is not merely the aggregate of all the finite objects which we observe or infer, but is a living whole, expressing itself in infinite variety. Of that infinite variety our gleams of consciousness are infinitesimal parts, but not parts in a sense involving any real division. The questions raised by such a view of the Universe, many of them unanswerable—as is also the case with questions raised by every other view of the Universe—will be considered further on. All that I

FOREWORD

am trying to secure in these preliminary observations is a general idea of the Pantheistic view of the Universe as distinguished from that of Polytheism, Monotheism, or Atheism.

Various Forms of Pantheism. Of course, there have been different forms of Pantheism, as there have been also various phases of Monotheism; and in the brief historical review which will follow this introductory explanation of the name, I shall note at least the most important of those forms. But any which fail to conform to the general definition here given, will not be recognised as Pantheism at all, though they may be worth some attention as approximations thereto.

Spurious Forms. For any view of the Universe, allowing the existence of anything outside the divine Unity, denies that God is All in All, and, therefore, is obviously not Pantheism. Whether we should recognise as true Pantheism any theory involving the evolution of a finite world or worlds out of the divine substance at some definite epoch or epochs, may be a debatable question, provided that the eternity and inviolability of the divine oneness is absolutely guarded in thought. Yet I will anticipate so far as to say that, in my view, the question must be negatived. At any rate,

PANTHEISM

Exclusion of Creation. we must exclude all creeds which tolerate the idea of a creation in the popular sense of the word, or of a final catastrophe. True, the individual objects, great or small, from a galaxy to a moth, which have to us apparently a separate existence, have all been evolved out of preceding modes of being, by a process which seems to us to involve a beginning, and to ensure an end. But in the view of Pantheism, properly so-called, the transference of such a process to the whole Universe is the result of an illusion suggested by false analogy. For the processes called evolution, though everywhere operative, affect, each of them, only parts of the infinite whole of things; and experience cannot possibly afford any justification for supposing that they affect the Universe itself. Thus, the matter or energy of which we think we consist, was in existence, every atom of it, and every element of force, before we were born, and will survive our apparent death. And the same thing, at least on the Pantheistic view, is true of every other mode of apparently separate or finite existence. Therefore no birth of a new nebula ever added a grain of matter or an impulse of new

Evolution and Decay applicable only to Parts, not to the Whole.

FOREWORD

energy to the Universe. And the final decease of our solar system, if such an event be in prospect, cannot make any difference whatever to the infinite balance of forces, of which, speaking in anthropomorphic and inadequate language, we suppose the Eternal All to consist.

Limitation of Scope. These observations are not intended to be controversial, but only to make clear the general sense in which the term Pantheism is here used. Not that it would be possible at the outset to indicate all that is implicit in the definition. I only wish to premise plainly that I am not concerned with any view of the world such as implies or admits that, whether by process of creation, or emanation, or self-division, or evolution, the oneness of the Eternal has ever been marred, or anything other than the being of God has been or can be produced.

But before passing on to the promised historical review, it is, perhaps, necessary to refer again to a **Pantheism either Philosophical or Religious or both.** remark previously made, that Pantheism may be considered either from the point of view of philosophy, or from that of religion. Not that the two points of view are mutually exclusive. But, as a matter of fact, Pantheism as a religion is, with certain exceptions among Indian saints and later Neoplatonists, almost entirely a modern development, of which Spinoza was the first distinct and devout teacher. For this statement justification will be given hereafter. Meantime, to deprecate adverse prejudice, I may suggest that a careful study of the most ancient forms of Pantheism seems to show that they were purely philosophical; an endeavour to reach in thought the ultimate reality which polytheism travestied, and which the senses disguised. But little or no attempt was made to substitute the contemplation of the Eternal for the worship of mediator divinities. Thus, in the same spirit in which Socrates ordered the sacrifice of a cock to Æsculapius for his recovery from the disease of mortal life, philosophical Pantheists, whether Egyptian or Greek, or even Indian,[1] satisfied their religious instincts by hearty communion with the popular worship of traditional gods. Or, if it is thought that the mediaeval mystics were religious Pantheists, a

Pantheism as a Religion almost Entirely Modern.

---

[1] If Buddha occurs to the reader, it should be remembered that he was not a Pantheist at all. His ultimate aim was the dissolution of personality in the Nothing. But that is not Pantheism.

FOREWORD

closer examination of their devout utterances will show that, though they approximated to Pantheism, and even used language such as, if interpreted logically, must have implied it, yet they carefully reserved articles of the ecclesiastical creed, entirely inconsistent with the fundamental position that there is nothing but God. Indeed, their favourite comparison of creature life to the ray of a candle is not really a Pantheistic conception; because to the true Pantheist the creature is not an emanation external to God, but a finite mode of infinite Being. Still the mystics did much to prepare the devout for an acceptance of Spinoza's teaching. And although so amazing a transfiguration of religion rather dazzled than convinced the world at first; nay, though it must be acknowledged that one, and perhaps more of Spinoza's fundamental conceptions have increasingly repelled rather than attracted religious people, yet it can hardly be disputed that he gave an impulse to contemplative religion, of which the effect is only now beginning to be fully realised.

Mystics not necessarily Pantheist.

CHAPTER I

PRE-CHRISTIAN PANTHEISM

Its Origins Doubtful and Unimportant. IT has been the customary and perhaps inevitable method of writers on Pantheism to trace its main idea back to the dreams of Vedic poets, the musings of Egyptian priests, and the speculations of the Greeks. But though it is undeniable that the divine unity of all Being was an almost necessary issue of earliest human thought upon the many and the one, yet the above method of treating Pantheism is to some extent misleading; and therefore caution is needed in using it. For the revival of Pantheism at the present day is much more a tangible resultant of action and reaction between Science and Religion than a ghost conjured up by speculation. Thus, religious belief, driven out from "the darkness and the cloud" of Sinai, takes refuge in the mystery of matter; and if the

PRE-CHRISTIAN PANTHEISM

glory passes from the Mount of Transfiguration, it is because it expands to etherialise the whole world as the garment of God. Again, the evanescence of the atom into galaxies of "electrons" destroys the only physical theory that ever threatened us with Atheism; and the infinitesimal electrons themselves open up an immeasurable perspective into the abyss of an Unknowable in which all things "live and move and have their being." Therefore it matters little to us, except as a matter of antiquarian interest, to know what the Vedic singers may have dreamed; or what Thales or Xenophanes or Parmenides may have thought about the first principle of things, or about the many and the one. For our spiritual genealogy is not from them, but from a nearer and double line of begetters, including seers—in the true sense of the word—and saints, for both are represented by Kepler and Hooker, Newton and Jeremy Taylor, Descartes and Spinoza, Leibnitz and Wesley, Spencer and Newman. And even these have authority not through any divine right of genius or acquired claim of learning, but because they illumine and interpret obscure suggestions of our own thoughts. Indeed, to the

The Secret of Pantheism is Within us.

sacrament of historic communion with the past, as well as to the chief rite of the Church, the apostolic injunction is applicable : "Let a man examine himself ; and so let him eat of that bread."

Obeying that injunction, any man possessing ordinary powers of observation and reflection may, in the course of a summer day's walk, find abundant reason for interest in the speculations of historic Pantheism. For the aspect of nature then presented to him is one both of movement and repose, of variety and harmony, of multiplicity and unity. Thus the slight breeze, scarcely stirring the drowsy flowers, the monotonous cadences of the stony brook, and the gliding of feathery flecks of cloud across the blue, create a peace far deeper than absolute stillness, and suggest an infinite life in which activity and repose are one. Besides, there is evident everywhere an interplay of forces acting and reacting so as mutually to help and fulfil one another. For instance, the falling leaves give back the carbon they gathered from the air, and so repay the soil with interest for the subtler essences derived therefrom and dissolved in the sap. The bees, again, humming among the

Suggestions of Nature.

flowers, while actuated only by instincts of appetite and thrift, fructify the blooms, and become a connecting link between one vegetable generation and another. The heat of the sun draws up water from ocean and river and lake, while chilly currents of higher air return it here and there in rain. So earth, sea, and air are for ever trafficking together; and their interchange of riches and force is complicated ten thousandfold by the activities of innumerable living things, all adapting themselves by some internal energy to the ever varying balance of heat and cold, moisture and drought, light and darkness, chemical action and reaction. And all this has been going on for untold millions of years; nor is there any sign of weariness now.

Sympathy thus awakened with the old Pantheistic Aspiration to find the One in the Many. In the mood engendered by such familiar experiences of a holiday saunter, it may well occur to anyone to think with interest and sympathy of the poets and seers who, thousands of years ago, first dared to discern in this maze of existence the varied expression of one all-embracing and eternal Life, or Power. Such contemplations and speculations were entirely uninfluenced by anything which the

PANTHEISM

Christian Church recognises as revelation.[1] Yet we must not on that account suppose that they were without religion, or pretended to explain anything without reference to superhuman beings called gods and demons. On the contrary, they, for the most part, shared, subject to such modifications as were imperatively required by cultivated common sense, the beliefs of their native land. But the difference between these men and their unthinking contemporaries lay in this; that the former conceived of one supreme and comprehensive divinity beyond the reach of common thought, an ultimate and eternal Being which included gods as well as nature within its unity. So, for them, Indra, Zeus, or Jove were mere modes of the one Being also manifest in man and bird and tree.

The Vedas and Related Literature. Every race possessing even the rudiments of culture has been impelled by a happy instinct, which, if we like, we may call inspiration, to record in more or less permanent form its experience of nature, of life,

---

[1] Some scholars think they can trace Christian influences in the exceptionally late Bhagavad Gîtâ, hereafter quoted. But it is a disputed point; and certainly in the case of the Vedas and pre-Christian literature arising out of them even Jewish influence was impossible.

PRE-CHRISTIAN PANTHEISM

and of what seemed the mysteries of both. To this inspiration we owe the sacred books of the Jews. But it is now generally recognised that an impulse not wholly dissimilar also moved prophetic or poetic minds among other races, such, for instance, as the Egyptians, the Chaldaeans, and the Aryan conquerors of India, to inscribe on papyrus or stone, or brick or palm-leaf, the results of experience as interpreted by free imagination, traditional habits of thought, and limited knowledge. Of this ancient literature a considerable part is taken up by the mysteries apparently involved in life, conduct, and death. Most notably is this the case with the ancient Indian literature called the Vedas, and such sequels as the Upanishads, Sutras, and—much later—the Bhagavad Gîtâ. This collection, like our Bible, forms a library of writings issued at various dates extending over much more than a thousand years.

The forgotten singers and preachers of this prehistoric wisdom were as much haunted as we ourselves are with the harassing questions suggested by sin and sorrow, by life and death, and by aspirations after a higher state. And many, perhaps *Indian Pantheism.* we may say most of them, found comfort in the thought that essentially they

PANTHEISM

belonged to an all comprehensive and infinite Life, in which, if they acted purely and nobly, their seeming personality might be merged and find peace. Their frame of mind was religious rather than philosophical. But their philosophy was naturally conformed to it; and in their contrast of the bewildering variety of finite visible things with the unity of the Eternal Being of which all are phases, those ancients were in close sympathy with the thoughts of the modern meditative saunterer by field and river and wood.

Differences between Ancient and Modern Conditions of Thought. But the enormous interval of time separating us from those early Indian thinkers necessarily involves very great differences in conditions of thought. And we should not be surprised if amidst much in their writings that stirs our sympathy, there is also a great deal which is to us incongruous and absurd. Therefore, it may be well before quoting these writings to note one or two points marking an almost incommensurable difference between their mode and ours of regarding the world.

1. Survival in their day of Fetishistic and Animistic Ideas. 1. First, they were much less removed than we are from the influence of fetishistic and animistic traditions. Even in the Greek and Roman classics

PRE-CHRISTIAN PANTHEISM

the casual reader is often revolted by the grossly absurd stories told of gods and heroes. And, indeed, it is impossible to conceive of the amours of Zeus (or Jove), for instance, with Leda, Europa or Danaë as having been first conceived during an age marked by the poetic genius and comparative culture evinced in the most ancient epics. But the most probable solution of the puzzle is that the earliest civilization inherited a number of animal stories, such as are characteristic of savagery in all parts of the world, and that the first literary generations into whose poetic myths those stories were transferred, being as much accustomed to them as to other surroundings of their childhood, such as bloody sacrifices, mystic expiations, and fantastic initiations, saw no incongruity in anything told them of the gods. Besides, as these wild myths were associated with sacred rites, the inveterate conservatism of religion, which insisted on stone knives in sacrifices long after bronze and iron came in, was likely enough to maintain the divine importance of those fables, just as the historicity of Balaam's ass and Jonah's whale is in some churches piously upheld still.

PANTHEISM

2. Ancient Ignorance of Natural Order. 2. In the times from which the first known Pantheistic teaching dates, ideas of nature's order were incongruous and indeed incommensurable with ours. Not that the world was then regarded as a chaos. But such order as existed was considered to be a kind of " balance of power" between various unseen beings, some good, some evil, some indifferent. True, some Indian prophets projected an idea of One Eternal Being including all such veiled Principalities and Powers. But their Pantheism was necessarily conditioned by their ignorance of natural phenomena. In fact, an irreducible inconsistency marred their view of the world. For while their Pantheism should have taught them to think of a universal life or energy as working within all things, their theological habit of mind bound them to the incongruous notion of devas or deities moulding, or at least ruling, matter from without. And, indeed, the nearest approach they made to the more genuine Pantheism of modern times was the conception of a world emanating from and projected outside Brahmă, to be re-merged in him after the lapse of ages. Now, if I am right in my definition of Pantheism as absolutely identifying God with the Universe,[1] so that, in fact, there cannot be anything but God, the inconsistency here noted must be regarded as fatal to the genuineness of the Indian or indeed of any other ancient Pantheism. For the defect proved during many centuries to be incurable, and was not indeed fully removed until Spinoza's time.

3. Absence of Definite Creeds.
3. Another difference between ancient Pantheists and ourselves was the absence in their case of any religious creed, sanctioned by supernatural authority and embodied in a definite form, like that of the three Anglican creeds, or the Westminster Confession of Faith. Not that those ancients supposed themselves to be without a revelation. For the Vedas, at least, were considered to be of divine authority, and their words, metres, and grammar were regarded with a superstitious awe, such as reminds us of what has been called the "bibliolatry" of the Jewish Rabbis. But subject to this verbal veneration, the Rishis, or learned divines, used

---

[1] As imperious brevity excludes full explanation, I must content myself with a reference to *The Religion of the Universe*, pp. 152–5. London: Macmillan & Co.

PANTHEISM

the utmost freedom in regard to the forced and fanciful interpretations extorted from the sacred text, a freedom which again reminds us of the paradoxical caprice shown by some schools of Jewish Rabbis in their treatment of the volume they professed to regard with awe. The various finite gods, such as Vishnu, Indra, Krishna, Marut, or Varuna, were not the subjects of any church creed chanted every day, and carefully stereotyped in the tender minds of children. On the contrary, various rôles were assigned by successive generations to these divinities. So that, for instance, Varuna was at one time the god of the ocean, and at another of the sky. But the uniform tendency of all poets and Rishis alike was to seek, beyond all these gods, one unbeginning, unending, and all comprehensive Being, from whom these "devas" emerged, and into whom they must return. Not only so, but it is clearly suggested in many passages, of which an instance will presently be quoted, that the Eternal, called Brahmă, who was the true Self of all gods, was also the true Self of man and bird and beast. So that, in fact, notwithstanding the illogical emanation theory, He was the only real Being, the All in All.

PRE-CHRISTIAN PANTHEISM

Illustration from the Upanishads. Thus, one section of the Khandogya Upanishad [1] consists entirely of instructions given by a father, Uddâlaka, to his son, Svetaketu, who had gone through the ordinary courses of study in the Vedas, but who, in the father's view, had failed to reach the true significance of life. Accordingly, Uddâlaka inquires: "Have you ever asked for that instruction by which we hear what cannot be heard, by which we perceive what cannot be perceived, by which we know what cannot be known?"[2] The youth, more accustomed than we are to teaching by paradox, expresses no surprise at this mode of putting things, but simply asks: "What is that instruction, sir?" The father then proceeds to give an explanation of what in these days is called **Monism.** "Monism," that is, the absolute singleness of ultimate Being, and traces all that is, or seems to be, up to one ultimate Essence. Now, whether in the form given by Uddâlaka to his

---

[1] According to the late Max Müller, with whom Prof. T. W. Rhys Davids agrees, the word Upanishad is equivalent to our word "sitting" or "session; only that it is usually confined to a sitting of master and pupil.

[2] *Sacred Books of the East*, vol. i. p. 92. The immediately following quotations are from the same Upanishad.

exposition, his theory can properly be called Pantheism, according to the definition of it assumed above, is perhaps questionable. But that it was intended to be Pantheism there can be no doubt. "In the beginning," says Uddâlaka, "there was that only which is (τὸ ὄν); one only, without a second. Others say, in the beginning there was that only which is not (τὸ μὴ ὄν); one only, without a second; and from that which is not, that which is was born." But Uddâlaka rejects this latter doctrine as unthinkable—which, indeed, many explorers of Hegel have found with pain and anguish of mind. And then the father traces all the multiformity of the Universe to the desire or will of the original One, "that which is." "It thought, 'may I be many; may I grow forth.' It sent forth fire." My limits do not allow me to quote further the fantastic account given of the farther process by which water and earth, plants, animals, and men sprang out of that desire of the One: "May I become many; may I grow forth." For our purpose it is more important to show that in the view of Uddâlaka—however inconsistently he may express himself—the original One was never really divided, but remains the true Self of every finite

Evolution from the One through Desire.

PRE-CHRISTIAN PANTHEISM

being, however apparently separate. Thus, consider the following dialogue, the first words being a direction of the father, Uddâlaka :—

"Fetch me from thence a fruit of the Nyagrodha tree." "Here is one, sir." "Break it." "It is broken, sir." "What do you see there ?" "These seeds, almost infinitesimal." "Break one of them." "It is broken, sir." "What do you see there ?" "Not anything, sir." The father said : "My son, that subtile essence which you do not perceive there, of that very essence this great Nyagrodha tree exists. Believe it, my son. That which is the subtile essence, in it all that exists has itself. It is the True. It is the Self; and thou, O Svetaketu, art it."

Here we are clearly taught that the "self," or inmost reality of every person and thing is the Eternal One, or Brahmă, or God.

Illustration from the Bhagavad Gitâ. The same doctrine is taught in a more advanced form by the poem called the "Bhagavad Gîtâ," the date of which is probably more than a thousand years later than that of the Upanishad just quoted. In this poem, Krishna, incarnate for the nonce as Arjuna's charioteer, reveals for a special purpose his identity with Brahmă, the

PANTHEISM

Eternal All; and Arjuna, when sufficiently instructed adores him thus :—

> "O infinite Lord of Gods! the world's abode,
> Thou undivided art, o'er all supreme.
> Thou art the first of Gods, the ancient Sire,
> The treasure-house supreme of all the worlds.
> The Knowing and the Known, the highest seat.
> From Thee the All has sprung, O boundless Form!
> Varuna, Vazu, Agni, Yama thou,[1]
> The Moon; the Sire and Grandsire too of men.
>
> The Infinite in power, of boundless force,
> The All thou dost embrace; the Thou art All." [2]

Omission of Buddhism. These illustrations must suffice for Indian Pantheism. Because, with Buddhism we have nothing to do. For, according to its ablest European exponent (Professor T. W. Rhys Davids), that system of religion simply ignored the conception of an All in All. And this not at all on philosophical grounds, but because its aims were entirely practical. For the aim of its founder was to show men how by a virtuous life, or lives, they might at last attain annihilation—or, at any rate, the extinction of

---

[1] "The gods of ocean, air and fire, and the judge of the lower regions respectively" (Rev. John Davies).
[2] The "Bhagavad Gîtâ," translated by the Rev. J. Davies, M.A.

PRE-CHRISTIAN PANTHEISM

the individual self, the apparent separateness of which was, in his view, the source of all misery. And if he could teach his followers to attain that salvation, he was entirely indifferent as to the opinions they might hold about the ultimate nature of the world, provided only that they did not fall into any heresy which proclaimed an immortal soul.[1]

Persian Religions, not strictly Pantheistic. The accounts given to us by the best authorities on Zoroaster and Parseeism scarcely justify us in thinking the religion of the Zendavesta to be Pantheistic in our sense of the term. For though it would appear that Ormuzd (or Ahuramazda), the God of light and goodness, originated in, or was born from and one with a nameless impersonal Unity, such as may answer to Herbert Spencer's "Unknowable," it cannot be accurately said that, according to the Persian view of the world, there is nothing but God. For, to say

---

[1] The Karma was *not* a soul. What it was is, according to our authorities, very difficult for the Western mind to conceive. But its practical effect was, that on the death of the imperfect man, another finite existence of some sort necessarily took his place. But this new finite existence was not the former man. It is only on the death of him who has attained Nirvana that Karma ceases to act, and no new finite existence takes his place.

PANTHEISM

nothing of the apparently independent existence of the principle of darkness and evil called Ahriman, the relation of the Amshaspands, or supreme spirits, and of the Izeds, or secondary spirits, as well as of the Fereurs, or divine ideas to the impersonal Unity, seems to be rather that of emanations, than parts of a Whole. Again, if it be true that, according to the Zend Avesta, the conflict of light and darkness will ultimately cease, and Ahriman with his demons be annihilated, it is obvious that this implies a beginning and an end, with a process originating in the one, and consummated in the other. But such a process, though most actual on the finite scale, and joyfully or painfully real to us, contemplating, as we do only infinitesimal parts of the Universe, and always under the forms of time and space, is yet incongruous and incommensurate with the thought of one All in All, unlimited by time or space, and whose lifetime is an Eternal Now. Thus true Pantheism takes the Universe, as it is, in its infinity; regards it as without beginning or end; and worships it. Not that Pantheism denies the existence of evil or is unmoved by the struggle between evil and good,

A World Drama or Process is a Human, not a Divine Aspect of of Things.

PRE-CHRISTIAN PANTHEISM

or is uninspired by faith in the reiterated triumph of good wherever the local conflict arises. But it insists that evil is relative to the finite parts of the Universe in their supposed isolation, and cannot possibly affect the Eternal All. It allows of no creation or emanation which would put any part of the "wondrous Whole" in opposition to, or separation from, the Eternal. But from its point of view all change, evolution, progress retrogression, sin, pain, or any other good or evil is local, finite, partial; while the infinite co-ordination of such infinitesimal movements make one eternal peace.

Pantheism in Ancient Egypt. Egyptian Religion need not detain us. For though there are clear traces of Pantheistic speculation among the Priests, it can scarcely be contended that such speculations had the same influence on the cultured laity as the teaching of the Rishis had in ancient India. But the truth seems to be that the oldest popular theology of Egypt was only a **Permanent Effects of Prehistoric Animism.** variety of Negro animism and fetishism.[1] Yet these grovelling superstitions, as is often the case, evolved in

[1] See Prof. W. Max Muller, on "Egypt," in the *Encyc. Biblica*.

PANTHEISM

unbroken continuity a higher faith. For, in the attempt made to adapt this savage cult to the religious needs of various districts, all alike gradually advancing in culture, the number and variety of divinities became so bewildering to the priests, that the latter almost inevitably adopted the device of recognising in parochial gods only so many hints of one all-comprehensive divine energy. Not that they ever embraced monotheism—or the belief in one personal God distinct from the Universe. But if Plutarch be accurate—as there seems no reason to doubt, in his record of an inscription in a temple of Isis—they, or at least the most spiritual of them, found refuge in Pantheism. For the transfigured and glorified goddess was not regarded as the maker of the Universe, but as identical with it, and therefore unknowable. "I am all that hath been, is, or shall be; and no mortal has lifted my veil." The prevalence of such Pantheism, at least among the learned and spiritual of ancient Egypt, is, to a considerable extent, confirmed by other Greek writers besides Plutarch. But the inscription noted by Plutarch gives the sum and substance of what they tell us.

[margin: Isis, according to Plutarch.]

PRE-CHRISTIAN PANTHEISM

Greek Pantheism
Before considering the classical and Neo-platonic Greek speculations commonly regarded as Pantheistic, we may do well to recall to mind the immense difference between the established habit of theological thought in our day, and the vague, or at best, poetically vivid ideas of the ancients. For the long tradition of nearly two thousand years, which has made monotheism to us almost as fixed an assumption as that of our own individuality, was entirely wanting in this case. Not that the idea of one supreme God had never been suggested.

Evolved from Polytheism.
But it was not the Hebrew or Christian idea that was occasionally propounded; for in the ethnic mind it was rarely, if ever, regarded as inconsistent with polytheism; and consequently it verged on Pantheism. "Consequently," I say, because such monotheism as existed had necessarily to explain the innumerable minor deities as emanations from, or manifestations of the supreme God. And though such conscious attempts at reconciliation of beliefs in many gods and in one Supreme were confined to a small minority of meditative priests and speculative philosophers, yet really, the combination was implicit in the sort of polytheistic religion

PANTHEISM

which possessed the family affections and patriotic associations of the early Greek world.

Not the Material Figure but the Divinity Suggested was the Object of Worship. For though we may find a difficulty in ridding ourselves of a prejudice wrought into the tissue of our early faith by the nursery lessons of childhood, it was not the graven or molten image which was really worshipped by the devout, but that form of superhuman power which, by local accident, had been identified with the "idol." If, indeed, we supposed every "idolator" to have received definite religious teaching, analogous to that with which we ourselves were imbued in youth, we might well find his attitude inconceivable. But he had nothing of the kind. He only knew that in war, in hunting, in fishing, in farming, he was confronted with powers which passed his comprehension; and tradition permeated him with the expectation that such powers would be propitiated by his worship of the images set up in their names. There was therefore no reasoned creed, such as those of the Catholic and Reformed Churches, but only a vague sentiment brought to a focus by the associations of the shrine. From such a view of polytheism it is easy to understand how most, if not all, of the old speculative philosophers could allow the existence of the traditional gods, even while in reasoned contemplation they saw that all deities were subordinate to and merged in one universal God.

Possible Influence of Oriental Pantheism. How far this unstable religious position was subject to the influence of the oriental mysticism at which we have glanced already, is, at any rate, so far as concerns the classical age of Greek philosophy, a matter of conjecture. But the resurrection of a prehistoric and almost forgotten civilization from the buried cities of Crete has brought to light many evidences of frequent intercourse, two or three thousand years before the Christian era, between European and Egyptian, or Asiatic, centres of life. Therefore, we may well believe that during the earliest stages of the evolution of thought in East and West, it was as impossible as at the present time for any local school of thinkers to be absolutely original or independent. Thus, later Greek philosophers, whether themselves within sound of the echoes of Hindoo teaching or not, may very well have grown up in an atmosphere impregnated with mythic germs,

PANTHEISM

whose origin they did not know. But however that may be, Greek Pantheism, while it had many points of contact with Eastern speculation, was more purely intellectual and less essentially religious than the Pantheism of the Vedas, or the solemn dream that haunted Egyptian temples. For while the aspiration of Hindoo Pantheists was to find and assume the right attitude toward "the glory of the sum of things," the Greeks, as St. Paul long afterward said, "sought after wisdom," and were fascinated by the idea of tracing all the bewildering variety of Nature up to some one "principle" ($ἀρχή$), beginning, origin.

Thales, about 640 B.C. Thus Thales of Miletus, during the late seventh and early sixth century B.C., is said to have been satisfied when he found in water—or moisture—the ultimate principle out of which all things and all life, including gods and men, were evolved. With such a speculation of infant philosophy we are here not concerned, except to say that it was not Pantheism as understood in modern times. For while his ablest exponents admit that no sufficient evidence is left to show very clearly what he meant, there seems no reason for supposing that to him the Universe was a Living God.

PRE-CHRISTIAN PANTHEISM

Successors of Thales. It would be fruitless to relate how successors of Thales varied his theory of an ultimate "principle," by substituting air or fire for water. But it is worth while to note that another citizen of Miletus, Anaximander, after an interval of some forty years, pronounced that the beginning, the first principle, the origin of all things, was neither water, nor air, nor fire, but the Infinite (τὸ ἄπειρον). And though the best authorities confess that they cannot be sure of his meaning, this may very well be because he anticipated Herbert Spencer by two and a half millenniums, in acknowledging that all things merge in one and the same Unknowable. But, so far as our evidence goes, he made no such attempt as the modern philosopher did, to persuade the religious instinct that this Unknowable could supply the place of all the gods.

Xenophanes of Elea, about 570 to 480 B.C. The position of Xenophanes, who, toward the latter part of the sixth century B.C. migrated, apparently for political reasons, in fear of Persian imperialism, from Colophon in Asia Minor to Elea in Italy, was a little different, and, for our purpose, more interesting. For the few fragments which are unfortunately all that is left to us of

PANTHEISM

his philosophical poetry, are strongly suggestive of Pantheism, and the interpretation put upon them by later classical and sub-classical writers, who had his works before them, would appear decisive. True, the distinguished and enlightened scholar, Simon Karsten, who, in the first quarter of the nineteenth century, found a labour of love in collecting and editing the remains of early Greek philosophers, deprecated such a judgment. Yet, while the motives for his special pleading were honourable, seeing the odious misrepresentations of Pantheism still prevalent in the Dutch scholar's native land,—misrepre-

His Pantheism Disputed but well Established. sentations undissipated even by the splendour of Spinoza,—his protest remains special pleading still. And he himself candidly quotes at large from an alleged work of Aristotle—possibly, only a student's notes of the latter's lectures—and also from Simplicius, as reported by Theophrastus in a comment on Aristotle's Physics, sentences which describe the system of Xenophanes as unquestionably Pantheistic. From which description I gather that the devout philosopher regarded

His Religion. God as the only real Being, including all that in human language has been, is, and will be, without beginning or end, living and perceiving equally everywhere throughout His infinite essence. And if that essence is compared by Xenophanes to a sphere, neither bounded nor boundless, neither moving nor immovable, this is only because few, if any, in that age of the world, could content themselves with loyally accepting the limits imposed on man by the very nature of things, limits which now compel us to own that, while the Eternal is more real than ourselves, yet, in the strict sense of knowing, He is, from an intellectual standpoint, the Unknowable.

Extent of his Sympathy with Popular Religion. This Pantheism did not generate in Xenophanes any arrogant disdain for the religion of his time. For, though he condemned, in words often quoted, the folly which supposed the gods to have the human form, senses, passions and appetites, he was yet glad to worship the divine All as partially manifested in finite beings—perhaps personfied powers of nature. *A Pantheistic Communion Feast.* Thus among the fragments of his poetry fortunately preserved, is one exquisite gem, a description of a festive repast in the open air. There purity comes first, symbolised by clear floor, clean hands, and spotless dishes. Upon

PANTHEISM

purity waits beauty, not in the forms desired by sensuous passion, but in garlands of flowers and in delicate scents. The wine is unstinted, yet tempered with sparkling water. But, lest the plentifulness of bread and honey and cheese upon the lordly table should eclipse the highest sanctions of human joy, an altar prominent in the festive scene is heaped with offerings of flowers. Then the first note of music is the praise of God, a praise taking form in blameless poetic myths and holy thoughts. In such a feast the minds of the guests are kindled with a desire to be capable of doing right. "There is no harm in drinking with reasonable moderation[1]; and we may honour the guest who, warmed by wine, talks of such noble deeds and instances of virtue as his memory may suggest. But let him not tell of Titan battles, or those of the giants or centaurs, the fictions of bygone days, nor yet of factious quarrels, nor gossip, that can serve no good end. Rather

---

[1] "Capability of walking home without help," is the limit quaintly fixed by the poet. To our modern feeling it seems rather wide. Yet, practically, it is the limit professedly observed by our publicans in serving their customers.

let us ever keep a good conscience towards the gods."[1]

Having given so much space to an ancient who seems to me specially interesting as a prophet of the ultimate apotheosis of earthly religions, I must be content to indicate, in a very few lines, the course of the Pantheistic tradition among the Greeks after his day. The arithmetical mysticism of Pythagoras has no bearing upon our subject.

Empedocles, Middle of Fifth Century B.C. Empedocles of Agrigentum, living about the middle of the fifth century B.C., and thus, perhaps, in the second generation after Xenophanes, was, in many respects, a much more imposing figure—clothed in purple, wielding political power, possessing medical skill, and even working miraculous cures, such as are apparently easy to men of personal impressiveness, sympathy, and "magnetism." But he does not appear to have so nearly anticipated modern Pantheism as did his humbler predecessor. For though the fragments of Empedocles, much larger in volume than those of Xenophanes,

---

[1] Karsten, *Xenophanis Reliquiae*, p. 68 (Amsterdam, 1830). Both the paraphrase and occasional translations which I give are of course free; but I think the spirit and meaning are preserved.

certainly hint at some kind of everlasting oneness in things, and expressly tell us that there is no creation nor annihilation, but only perpetual changes of arrangement, yet they present other phases of thought, apparently irreconcileable with the doctrine that there is nothing other than God. Thus he teaches that there are four elements—earth, air, water and fire—out of which all things are generated. He also anticipates Lucretius in his pessimistic view of humanity's lot; and insists on the apparently independent existence of a principle of discord or strife in the Universe. It would be a forced interpretation to suppose him to have set forth precociously the Darwinian theory of the struggle for life. For his notion seems much more akin to the Zoroastrian imagination of Ahriman. Again, he sings melodiously, but most unphilosophically, of a former golden age, in which the lion and the lamb would seem to have lain down together in peace; and trees yielded fruit all the year round. At that time the only deity was Venus, who was worshipped with bloodless offerings alone. Still, it must be remembered that, whether consistently or not, Empedocles produced an elaborate work on the Nature of Things, to which Lucretius makes eloquent and earnest acknowledgments. But that very approval of Lucretius forbids us to regard the older poet as a Pantheist in our sense of the term. For certainly to him the Universe cannot have been a living God.

Not Properly a Pantheist.

Genesis of Modern Religious Pantheism. Between this philosophical idea of a Oneness, not thought of as God, and the spiritual contemplation of a universal Life of which all things are modes, the highest thoughts of men hovered during the process by which, in some measure under extraneous influences, Greek speculation finally produced Neo-platonism—or, as we might say in the current phraseology of our time—a restatement of Plato's teaching. Of this school, arising in the early Christian centuries, some leaders were undoubtedly Pantheists. But we cannot say this of Plato himself, nor of his master Socrates. For though these great men were more profoundly interested in the moral order of the world than in any questions of physical nature, or even of metaphysical subtleties, they were never given to the kind of contemplation suggested above in extracts from the Classical Books of the East, the contemplation which educes the moral ideal from unre-

PANTHEISM

served subordination of self to the Universe as of the part to the Whole. Doubtless the inspiration imparted by Socrates to a disciple in mere intellect his superior, and the resulting moral and religious suggestions abounding in the Dialogues, did much to impel the current of religious evolution toward that spiritual aspect of the Infinite All which fascinated some of the Neo-Platonists, and received its most splendid exposition from Spinoza. But the conditions imposed by necessary brevity compel me to pass by those classic names with this acknowledgment, and to hasten toward the fuller revelation of Pantheism as a religion.

CHAPTER II

POST-CHRISTIAN PANTHEISM.

In speaking of Neo-Platonism I incidentally mentioned its apparent subjection to " extraneous influences." These, of course, included the rising power of Christianity and its Jewish traditions. **The Hebrew Tradition.** Even before the advent of the new revelation, the Jewish settlements existing in all great cities of the Graeco-Roman world excited interest at any rate among sentimentalists touched by the fascination at that time beginning to be exerted by oriental religions. And this influence of Jewish traditions was much facilitated by the existence of a Greek translation of the Hebrew scriptures.

Now, what the Hebrew tradition did for Greek **Its Influence on Greek Philosophy.** philosophy was, of course, not to favour its Pantheistic trend, where that existed, but much more to convert such semi-Pantheism from a mere intel-

PANTHEISM

lectual speculation to contemplative devotion. For Hebraism itself had become almost as intensely monotheistic as the later Islam. And,

To Inspire Devotion, Not Solve Problems. though monotheism may be a stage in the progress of religion from Animism to Pantheism, it may, also, by the peculiar intensity of the personal devotion it sometimes inspires, cause the very idea of any farther expansion of faith to be counted a sin.

Perhaps the influence of Hebraism on Hellenism may be illustrated by the Alexandrian

Philo, the Jew of Alexandria. Philo's pathetic endeavour not only to trace the wisdom of the Greeks to Moses, but to show that this derived lore is much mightier for good when re-invested with the spiritual power and ardent devotion of the Jewish faith.

"If any one will speak plainly," he writes,[1] "he might say that the intelligible world is nothing other than the word (sc. λόγος, reason) of the world-making God. For neither is the intelligible city anything other than the thought (λογισμός) of the architect already intending to

[1] *De Mundi Opificio*, p. 5B. I take him to mean by κόσμος νοητός—the world as apperceived—realised in our consciousness.

POST-CHRISTIAN PANTHEISM

build the city. This is the teaching of Moses, not mine. At any rate in what follows, when he records the origin of man, he declares outright that man was made in the image of God. But if a part (of creation) reflects the type, so also must the entire manifestation, this intelligible ordered world, which is a reproduction of the divine image on a larger scale than that of man." [1]

How Philo managed to extort this out of the Pentateuch is a question of interest, but one on which I cannot delay. Suffice it, that while he thus showed his reverence for the traditions of his race, his whole aim is to fire philosophy with religious devotion. But he was not, in any strict sense of the word, a Pantheist, though he regarded the Logos as an emanation from the Eternal, and the kosmos, the ordered world, as in some way emanating from the Logos. Perhaps, indeed, if we could exclude from emanation the idea of time,

Motives Underlying his Distortion of Hebraism.

---

[1] It should be noted that Philo, who was contemporary with Jesus, often uses the title "the Father" (ὁ Πατήρ) as a sufficient designation of the Eternal. It was not very usual, and is suggestive of certain spiritual sympathies amidst enormous intellectual divergencies between the Alexandrian philosopher and the Galilean prophet.

PANTHEISM

Not Pantheistic. as Christians are supposed to do when they speak of the "eternal generation" of the Divine Son or the "procession" of the Holy Ghost, we might regard Philo, with the succeeding Neo-Platonists and some of the Gnostics, as approximately Pantheistic. But his vagueness and uncertainty about matter forbid such a conclusion. For whether he regarded matter as eternally existing apart from the divine substance, or whether he looked upon it as the opposite of Being, as a sort of positive nothing, in either case, it cannot be said that for him the whole Universe was God, and nothing but God.

If I have given more space to the great Alexandrian Jew than my narrow limits ought to afford, it is because I think I may thus avoid the necessity of saying much about the philosophic **Neo-Platonism.** schemes of the Neo-Platonists, the phantasies of the Gnostics, or the occasionally daring speculations of the Christian Fathers. For whether the works of Philo were much studied by the Greeks or not, they certainly **Resultant of Contact between East and West.** described the spiritual resultant—so to speak—emerging from the mutual impact of Western and Oriental, especially Jewish, ideas. Which resultant was "in the air" from the first century of the Christian age; and the later epistles ascribed to St. Paul, as well as the Fourth Gospel, show clear traces of it.[1]

But the inspiration of the time-spirit was not confined to the Christian Church. For the city of Alexandria, where that spirit seems to have been peculiarly potent as shown in the transfigured Judaism of Philo, was the birthplace of the Neo-Platonic school already mentioned above. And among its greatest members, such as Plotinus, Porphyry, Proclus, the religious influence of the East was distinctly apparent. True, they followed Socrates and Plato in reverence for knowledge as the unfailing begetter of virtue. But their speculations about the divine Being were touched by Oriental emotion. And we may with some confidence believe that their development of the Platonic Trinity owed a good deal to the rapid spread of Christianity. Thus the sentiment, the fervour, the yearning for "salvation," the worship and devotion taught by the best of the Neo-Platonists

Its Religious Inspiration.

---

[1] See Col. i. 15–17 and refs. John i. 1–3; iii. 13; viii. 58.

PANTHEISM

were not so much from Athens as from Sinai and Galilee. Yet, though there were in their world-conception many anticipations of the gospel of the "God-intoxicated man," whom the counsels of the Eternal reserved for the fulness of times, it would scarcely be accurate to describe the system of any of them as strictly Pantheistic. For they were always troubled about "matter" as an anomalous thing in a divine universe, and in treating of it they hesitated between the notion of an eternal nuisance which the Demiurgus, or acting God, could only modify, not destroy, and, on the other hand, a strained theory of an evil nothing, which is yet something. Again, so far from realising Spinoza's faith in God as so literally All in All that there is nothing else but He, they would not tolerate the contact of the Infinite with the finite, of God with the world. Consistently with such prepossessions, they held obstinately to the notion of some beginning, and therefore some ending of the ordered world. And this beginning was effected by emanations such as the Logos, or, as others had it, the world-soul and other divine energies, between the Eternal and creation; a

Suggestive of Pantheism, but not such in Spinoza's Sense.

POST-CHRISTIAN PANTHEISM

phantasy which, however poetically wrought out, is not really consistent with Pantheism.

Such ideas of a hierarchy of subordinate emanations to fill the supposed abyss between the Infinite and the Finite were eagerly adopted and developed by the pseudo-philosophers called Gnostics, on both sides of the boundary between the Church and the World. Suffice it that, like most, though by no means all of their predecessors, they regarded the world of earth, sun, planet, stars, and animated nature with man at its head, as the whole Universe; and, assuming that it must have had a beginning, they vexed their souls with futile attempts to frame some gradual transition from the uncreated to the created, from the eternal to the mortal. The grotesque chimaeras engendered thus are remembered now only as illustrations of the facile transition from the sublime to the ridiculous and from philosophy to folly.

[margin: The Gnostics.]

The orthodox Christian fathers were not less conscious than the Neo-Platonists or Gnostics of the perennial problem of the Many and the One. But they were restrained, perhaps, by the "faith that comes of self-control," perhaps by mere common sense, from indulging

[margin: The Church Fathers.]

PANTHEISM

in attempts to connect the Infinite with the Finite by "vain genealogies." Indeed, for the most part they confessed that whatever light the Gospel might shed on moral issues, it left untouched the ultimate question of the relation of the Infinite to the Finite. And the only aspect of their most venturesome speculations which I need recall is their insistence, even when apparently verging toward Pantheism, on a transcendent as well as an immanent God, that is on a Creator existing, so to speak, outside the Universe and apart from it as well as permeating every part. Thus, for example, Augustine would seem to deny to the world any separate creature existence when he says, that but for the divinity everywhere in it, creation would cease to be. But in his insistence on the creation of the world from nothing, he directly contradicts Pantheism, because he must necessarily be taken to mean that there is now something other than God.

Augustine.

That there have been devout Christians whose mystic speculations on the relations of the soul to the Eternal logically involved Pantheism—if logic in such a case had any function—there can be no doubt. But for most of them "God's word written" seemed to confirm God's word in

POST-CHRISTIAN PANTHEISM

heaven and earth as known to them, proclaiming that there had been a beginning and there must be an end. Therefore, whatever might be the immanence of the Creator in His works, God could not, in their minds, be identified with " the fashion of this world " which " passeth away."

Yet the time was coming when the Divine word both in Scripture and in Nature was to be otherwise read. For men began to learn that the Bible was other than they had supposed and the Universe immeasurably greater than they had conceived.

CHAPTER III

MODERN PANTHEISM.

Spinoza. MODERN Pantheism as a religion begins with Spinoza. Whether it ended with him is a question which the future will have to decide. But the signs of the times are, at least in my view, very clearly against such a conclusion. And amongst the omens which portend immortality, not necessarily for the philosophical scheme, but for the "God-intoxicated" devoutness of his Pantheism, is the desire, or rather the imperious need increasingly realized, for a religion emancipated from theories of creation or teleology, intolerant of any miracle, save indeed the wonders of the spiritual life, **A Pantheistic Prophet.** and satisfying the heart with an ever present God. For it is to be remembered that Spinoza was the first Pantheist who was also a prophet, in the sense of speaking out the divine voice of the infinite Universe to its human constituent parts. Not that I would minimize the religious fervour of the Neo-Platonists: it is their Pantheism that seems to have been imperfect. But in Spinoza we have a man who, inheriting by birth the tradition—I might even say the apostolic succession—of the Jewish prophets, and gifted with an insight into the consummation of that tradition in Jesus Christ, was driven by a commanding intellect to divorce the spiritual life he prized from creeds that had become to him impossible, and to enshrine it in the worthier temple of an eternal Universe identical with God. It is not, then, with his philosophy that I am so much concerned as with his religion.[1]

The Main Subject here is his Religion and not his Philosophy.

---

[1] It is not within the scope of the present essay to give a life of Baruch (or Benedict) de Spinoza. But for the sake of those to whom the work of Sir Frederick Pollock is not easily accessible, the following particulars may be given. Spinoza was born in Amsterdam, November, 1632, of a fairly prosperous Jewish family, originally from Portugal. He received thorough instruction in the language and literature of the Hebrews, and in addition became a good Latin scholar, so far as to write and correspond in that language. He was early interested in philosophy, and especially attracted for a

PANTHEISM

It is given to no man to be absolutely original in the sense of creating ideas of which no germs existed before his day. But short of such an impossible independence of the past, Benedict de Spinoza had perhaps as much originality as any man who ever lived. Yet with a modesty ever characteristic of moral greatness, he himself was disposed, at any rate during his earlier philosophical development, to

His Originality.

time by the writings of Descartes. By the time he was twenty-three years old he was suspected of heresy, and in his twenty-fourth year (1655) was cut off from the Synagogue with a frightful curse. His family disowned him, and for his maintenance he turned to the polishing of lenses, a trade already learned in accordance with the Jewish custom that every boy must have a handicraft. What he earned would hardly be considered a "living wage" in these days. But according to Colerus, his first biographer, who enquired of the householders with whom Spinoza lodged, his day's maintenance often cost no more than 4½d. Various incidents proved his total indifference to money, except as far as needed to "provide things honest in the sight of all men." Though of an amiable and sociable disposition he lived a solitary life, while not indisposed to kindly talk with his humbler neighbours. He had some of the greatest scholars of the day among his correspondents. He published but little during his life, leaving his greatest work as a legacy to the world on his early death, at the Hague, from consumption, in 1677.

MODERN PANTHEISM

Relation to Descartes. exaggerate his indebtedness to the philosopher Descartes, whose system he laboriously abridged in the inappropriate form of a series of propositions supposed to be demonstrated after the fashion of Euclid.

But whatever may have been the esoteric belief of Descartes about creation out of nothing and the theological dogmas connected therewith, he **Fundamental Differences.** attached too much importance to the social and political functions of established ecclesiastical institutions to declare himself independent of them. And though his submission, signalised on his death-bed, did not interfere with the freest working of his brilliant intellect within limits permitted to the former ecclesiastical "schoolmen," it did prevent his frank realization of the eternal oneness of all being. For it compelled him to retain belief in a Creator distinct in essence from Creation. Such **Spinoza Discards Creator and Creation,** a belief Spinoza entirely rejected. For though his "Natura Naturans," or Nature Active, may in a manner be called the Creator of his "Natura Naturata," or Nature Passive, these are consubstantial and co-**Beginning and End.** eternal, neither being before or after the other. Thus for him there was no

PANTHEISM

beginning of the Universe and there could be no end. There was no creation out of nothing, nor any omen of weariness, decay, or death in the eternal order. He teaches us in effect to take the Universe as it is, and to pry into no supposed secrets of origin or end, an entirely gratuitous labour, imposed by illusions arising out of the continuous redistribution of parts of the Whole. Instead of thus spending our mental energy for nought, he would have us regard the whole of Being as one Substance characterized by innumerable attributes, of which Extension and Thought alone come within our human cognizance; while each Attribute is subject to infinite Modes or modifications, which, in their effect on the two attributes known to us —extension and thought—constitute the universe of our experience. That infinite and eternal Substance revealed by Attributes and their Modes is God, absolute in His perfections if He could be fully conceived and known in all His activities. And even to our ignorance He is entrancing in His gradual self-revelation, as with our inadequate ideas we pursue the unattainable from glory to glory.

Takes the Universe as it is.

And Worships the Static Whole as God.

MODERN PANTHEISM

This View of the Universe applied to Psalm civ.
This, then, is the first note we make of the gospel of Spinoza. But if any one thinks that the sacred word "gospel" is here misused, and that such teaching is fatal to piety, let him turn to the 104th Psalm and read, from Spinoza's point of view, the cosmic vision of the Hebrew seer. True, we can think no longer of the supernatural carpenter who works on "the beams of his chambers" above, or of the mythical engineer who digs deep in the darkness to "lay the foundations of the earth." For that is poetry, appealing by concrete images to the emotions. But it does not bind the intellect to a literal interpretation; and we are no longer tormented by vain efforts to reconcile with infinite impossibilities the half-human personality presented in poetic guise. So that the vision of the seer is now the suggestion to us of an infinite and eternal Being, whose attributes by modification take the innumerable shapes of sun, moon, and stars, and mountains and river, and tree and flower, and bird and beast, and man. And the winds that sweep and the floods that roll, and the rocky barriers that stand fast, and the rivers that wind among the hills, and the trees that flourish and

the living societies that gather in fruitful places, the labourer in his vineyard, the sailor in his ship, all are in and of the one Eternal Being. Yet we echo not with less, but perhaps with more reverence, than the believers in a divine artisan, the words of the Psalmist: "O Lord, how manifold are Thy works! in wisdom hast Thou made them all: the earth is full of Thy riches." But if the thunder and the flaming fire and the sweeping flood seem discordant, they existed for the Psalmist as well as for us, and they do not seem to have troubled him. At this point, therefore, we need only say that Spinoza's religion of one divine Substance, whose unity in variety is holy, ought to stir within us with not less fervour, at least the spirit of the Psalmist's concluding prayer: "Let the sinners be consumed out of the earth and let the wicked be no more."

Spinoza no Materialist. Spinoza's maintenance of extension as one of the two infinite divine attributes cognizable by us has, with a certain amount of plausibility, been urged as a note of materialism. And this reproach has been supported by reference to his insistence that in man the body and the soul are only two different aspects of the same thing; for to him

Notwithstanding his Attribution of "Extension" to God. the body is a finite Mode of God's infinite attribute of extension and the soul a finite Mode of God's infinite attribute of thought, while both are manifestations of the one eternal divine Substance. Still, if in any way we are to regard God as extended, it seems impossible to avoid the inference that we regard Him as identified with matter, or at least the possibility of matter.

Criticism by Sir F. Pollock. Sir Frederick Pollock has admitted that this is a weak point in Spinoza's philosophy,[1] and mars its symmetry. But, being more concerned with his religion, I am content to point out that such an objection was much **Changes in Theories of Matter since Spinoza's time.** more effective in Spinoza's time than it is to-day. For the whole trend of philosophy during the nineteenth century was towards a view of Extension itself as a mode of Thought, and therefore toward the absorption of one of Spinoza's theoretical divine attributes in the other.

---

[1] "It is to be observed that, inasmuch as Attribute is defined by reference to intellect, and Thought itself is an attribute, Thought appears to be in a manner, counted twice over."—*Spinoza: His Life and Philosophy*, by Sir Frederick Pollock. Second edition, 1899, p. 153.

PANTHEISM

Their Effect on his System.
Now if this should prove to be the permanent tendency of the most influential thinkers—as indeed seems most likely—it will probably be held that Spinoza was wrong in attributing extension to the Eternal as one of the qualities of His substance, except in so far as extension is, if not a necessary, at any rate an actual, and so far as we know, a universal mode of thought. But though, as Sir Frederick Pollock has pointed out, Spinoza has in a manner "counted thought twice over" while treating of the only two infinite attributes cognizable to us, we need not, on that account, surrender his luminous idea of God as a Being absolutely infinite, that is, "Substance consisting of infinite Attributes, whereof each one expresses eternal and infinite being." Nor need we abandon his supplementary but essential idea of "Modes" or "modifications" which mould the attributes into the varieties of finite worlds, known and unknown. Thus it may be that, in Spinoza's sense of the word "Attribute," we shall have to confess that only one comes within our human ken, that of Thought in a sense which includes feeling. But if the late Herbert Spencer, apart from his synthetic philosophy of

phenomena, has left any permanent mark on the religious consciousness, it has been by a consecration of the mystery of the ultimate Unknowable.[1] And in the spirit of reverence thus taught by him we may still hold with Spinoza that the Eternal has an infinity of other attributes with their infinite modifications not within our cognizance. This would only be an enlarged application of Hamlet's words :

"There are more things in Heaven and Earth, Horatio,
Than are dreamt of in your philosophy."

Or, to put it in another way, the Universe perceptible to us is only one of an infinity of Universes. By which is not meant an infinite

[1] It is of course true that Spinoza considered himself to have a clear and adequate conception of God. But by this he meant only that, as a philosopher, he had an intuitive certainty of eternal and infinite Being. So have all of us humbler mortals, though we should not have been able to express it for ourselves. No one supposes that for an indefinite space of time or eternity there was nothing, and then suddenly there was something. But, if not, then everyone recognises with Spinoza the fact of eternal Being, though, of course, he saw what this recognition meant, as the many do not. But when it comes to the facts of mortal imperfections and ignorance, Spinoza, with his theory of " inadequate ideas," is as ready as Spencer to acknowledge the Unknowable.

extension of galaxies in space, but the co-existence and, so to speak, interpenetration of an infinity of modes of existence imperceptible to us.

God is Identical with the Whole of Being. To Spinoza, then, God is the totality of Being. But it is not to be inferred that he identified God with the visible, or with any conceivable Universe. For either of these must fall far short of infinity, and the Being of God is infinite. All I mean, when I say that Spinoza identifies God with the totality of existence, is that he regards the deity as that Perfect Being without beginning or end, whose essence it is to be, and of whom all that exists, whether known to us or not, is separately a partial, and comprehensively a perfect expression.

His Doctrine of Man. Of more practical interest to us perhaps is Spinoza's doctrine of man, though it would have been impossible to explain that without first indicating his idea of God. In his view, then, man is a finite mode of the two divine attributes, extension and thought. Thus both the extended body and the conscious mind have their substance and reality in God.[1] But the essence of man does

---

[1] I do not think it necessary in an essay of this kind to discuss Spinoza's theory of the body as object of the

not necessarily involve his separate existence as the essence of God implies Being. Of course the substance of man is imperishable because it is of God's substance. Nay, there is a sense in which each man, being an eternal thought of God, has an aspect towards eternity or exists "sub specie eternitatis." But that is a truth transcending the finite practical world with which we have to do.

According to Spinoza, what constitutes the real essence of the human mind is the (divine) idea of a certain individual creature actually existing.[1] Here, perhaps, modern speculations

---

mind, and the mind as "idea" of the body, both being different aspects of the same thing.

"Rei alicujus singularis actu existentis." The word "divine" does not occur in Prop. xi. Ethices II., from which I quote. But it is implied; because the mind is only a mode or modification of the infinite attribute of thought, which again expresses the eternal Substance in God. I venture a doubt whether "actually existing," though adopted by such authorities as Sir F. Pollock gives, with any distinctness, Spinoza's meaning. I may be wrong, but I suspect that one of the later uses of "actus," as quoted in Ducange, affected Spinoza's Latinity. Thus several ecclesiastical writers are quoted as using the word in the sense of office, or function. Surely this would suit Spinoza's definition of the mind. For he treats it as a centre of phenomenal activity amidst

PANTHEISM

...about the constitution of matter may... if we use them with due reserve— Spinoza's notion of a "res singularis i[n]... or as it might be rendered freely, "[a ...] Illustration of individual functions," fo[r ...] by the called the "vortex theory[...] Vortex Theory — as old as Cartesian philoso[phy ...] recently flashed into sudden prominen[ce ...] whether or no the speculation be only [a ...] phase of human thought about the Un[iverse ...] it equally answers the purpose of ill[ustration.] Thus the so-called "ether" is suppose[d ...] space — and within it there are imagi[ned] form — innumerable "tourbillons" or "[vortices,"] which though parts of the indefinitely [extended] ether form by their self-contained mo[tion] worlds in themselves. These little wor[lds are] some regarded as the atoms which, [by their] position and differentiation, build up [the] palpable universe. With the possibiliti[es of] a theory I have nothing to do. But th[e ...]

... the infinite modes of the divine attribute. [...] individuality is a consequence of its spont[aneity ...] centre of action—always understood tha[t this spon-] taneity is consistent with the absolute e[ternity] assumed throughout the work.

the vortex in the ether may perhaps help us to a glimpse of Spinoza's notion when he speaks of a " res singularis in actu " a creature of individual functions. For to him man was, as it were, an infinitesimal vortex in a phase or attribute of the divine Substance. The analogy, like all other analogies, would not bear being pressed. But it does suggest to us a picture of finite individuality in action or function, subordinated to unity with infinite Substance. If it be said that

Distinction between Man and Beast. such an explanation would necessarily include the conscious life of beasts and birds, the answer would seem to be, that admitting this to be the case, yet in man the divine idea of individuality is more fully expressed and has more of reality than in any lower creature.

Moral Difficulties. Man, then, according to Spinoza, is in God and of God. But what are we to say of bad men, the vile, the base, the liar, the murderer? Are they also in God and of God? Spinoza does not blench. Yes, they are. But here comes in his doctrine of "adequate" and "inadequate ideas." Thus, if you see the colour red it completely expresses itself. It cannot be defined and needs no explanation.¹ As it is in the Infinite Thought so it is in ours. We have an "adequate idea" of it. But now if you see on an artist's canvas a splotch of red and blue and yellow, part of a work only begun, it gives you no adequate idea. True, you have an adequate idea of each several colour, but not of their relations to the work conceived. To get that you would have to enter into the mind of the artist and see as he sees. Then the splotch of colour would take its place as part of a harmonious whole; and would give you an adequate idea just as it does to the artist.

Now, according to Spinoza, when we see things as they appear in Infinite Thought we have an adequate idea. But if we see only a component element in an idea—let us say—of the divine Artist, then our idea is inadequate.²

---

¹ Of course the professor of optics can tell us how many vibrations in a second go to produce the particular shade of colour. But these cannot by any means be identified with conscious perception; and it is with this only that we are concerned.

² Ethices Pars II., Prop. xi. Corollarium. "Hence it follows that the human mind is part of the infinite intellect (thought) of God; and accordingly, when we say that the human mind perceives this or that, we only say that God—not in His infinity, but so far as He is expressed by the nature of the human mind, or, so far as He con-

MODERN PANTHEISM

Hence we misjudge things. And of the part played by bad men in the divine Whole we certainly have no adequate idea. But here again we must be on our guard against the abuse of illustrations. For it is not to be inferred that Spinoza regards the Universe as an unfinished picture, of which the completion will justify the beginning. On the contrary, the Universe is to him eternal, the necessary expression of the infinite attributes of eternal Being. Still the analogy may help us. For the concentration of attention on a single part of an ordered whole may, quite as certainly as a glance at an unfinished work,

<small>But the Universe is Not an Unfinished Picture.</small>

---

stitutes the essence of the human mind—has this or that idea. And when we say that God has this or that idea, not only so far as He constitutes the nature of the human mind, but so far as He has the idea also of some other thing together with the human mind, then we say that the human mind perceives the thing in part, or inadequately." E.G. all races have naturally supposed earthquakes and storm, battle, murder and sudden death to present ideas identical in the minds of their gods and of themselves. But Spinoza's suggestion, as I interpret it, is that the true God has the idea of such things, not only so far as He constitutes the human mind, but as He includes the ideas of some correlated things to us inconceivable. Our idea is therefore "inadequate."

be the occasion of an inadequate idea. In effect, the suggestion is that if we, like God, could contemplate the infinite Universe all at once, and have an adequate idea thereof, in other words if we could ascend to the self contemplation of the Eternal, we should have the bliss associated by long habit with the words of the Psalmist: "I shall be satisfied when I awake, with thy likeness." Such bliss, however, is only approximately attainable in moments of mystic transport. And when, as in so many experiences, we see only in part, and have inadequate ideas, faith in the Eternal Whole is needed to keep us from blasphemy.

It is an Eternal Whole, of which a Partial Consideration is Misleading.

With such necessarily brief hints as to Spinoza's attitude towards evil, I resume his doctrine of man—the individual creature as a centre of action. Of final causes Spinoza will not hear. But if instead of asking "what is the chief end of man," we ask what is the idea of man, Spinoza answers that it is the realization of a mode of the divine attributes, extension and thought. And if this should seem unsatisfying, let it be remembered that to this

Doctrine of Man Resumed.

Final Cause Replaced by Idea.

devout Pantheist the divine attributes and their modes were the expression of the very substance and life of God. Now with "extension," for reasons already given, we need not trouble ourselves except to say that at least Spinoza's teaching would suggest the idea of *mens sana in corpore sano*. Because to him the mind was the "idea" of the body, and the body the "object"—not quite in the modern sense—of the mind. But as regards the human mode of the divine attribute of thought, Spinoza makes its ideal to be a life absorbed in such contemplation of "the Blessed God," the infinite Whole, as shall react on the creature in inspirations of freedom, purity and love.

Freedom, Purity, Love.

Idea of Freedom. And first as to freedom, Spinoza means by this not caprice, nor the monstrous miracle of causeless action, but independence of external force or of any disproportionate and illegitimate passion. The freedom to which he aspires is the freedom of God, who eternally acts in accordance with the mutual harmony of the whole attributes of His nature, not one of which clashes with another. So Spinoza's free man is one in whom all aspirations

PANTHEISM

and energies, converging in one resultant, the expression of the divine idea, move him in harmony with the Universe. From such a point of view the quibbles about "free will," in the sense of causeless action, cease to have any meaning. For if the good man says "I could have done otherwise if I had liked," the obvious reply is, "Yes, but you would not have liked." Because the will is not a separate faculty, but the expression of the whole nature, as that exists at the moment of "willing." And the only real freedom is the unimpeded conglomerate impulse to do right. But should it be asked what if the resultant impulse of the whole nature is toward wrong? the answer is, in that case there is no freedom, but a slavery to some external influence or to a disturbed balance of the passions. Or if it be asked what is right? that is a far reaching question to the solution of which Spinoza bends all his splendid powers. But limits of space preclude me from saying more than that his ideal of right will be found conformable to the highest standards of the most spiritual religions.

Purity. This ideal I ventured to symbolize rather than define as "purity." For after all the philosophic reasoning with which it is no less lucidly than laboriously worked out in the final book of his *Ethica*, "Concerning Human Freedom"—the moral result of all this intellectual effort is that same cleansing of the soul from vain desire and that subordination of the earthly self to its divine idea which we are taught in the Sermon on the Mount. And while surely every one but a fanatical anti-Christian must allow the greater prophetic worth of the Galilean, who could teach these sublime lessons so that "the common people heard him gladly," it seems difficult to deny to the heretic Jew of the Hague the second rank among the teachers given to the world by that strangely gifted race. For though he could not speak to "the common people," he left as his legacy to mankind, not so much a system of philosophy, as an impregnable foundation for morals and religion, available for the time now coming upon us—such a time as that suggested by the writer of the Epistle to the Hebrews, when he spoke of "the removing of those things that are shaken, as of things that are made, that those things which cannot be shaken may remain." No doubt Sir Frederic Pollock is quite right in declaring that Spinoza would have been the very last man to desire any one to become a Spinozist. But that is quite consistent with the inspired Pantheist's infinite longing to see all men blessed by that inward peace which he proved, by his own heroic experience, to be identical with the self-control conferred and maintained by devout contemplation of God's all-comprehensive Being and our place therein. If, then, I regard purity as the best symbol of such a moral ideal, it is because the word connotes, together with freedom from discordant passion, a frankly unconstrained recognition of the simplicity of our relation to God. For surely when once the self has made the great surrender, and becomes content to be nothing, that in St. Paul's words, "God may be all in all," the whole problem of life is infinitely simplified, in the sense that no farther degree of simplification is possible. Because all contradictions of pain and evil and sorrow are dissolved in that act of surrender. We must, indeed, recognize that to our "inadequate ideas" the time often seems "out of joint." But we need not, with Hamlet, cry out on an impossible "spite." For when once it is heartily and loyally realized that not our partial likings, but the eternal harmony of the Whole, is the glory of God, we already anticipate the peace of absorption in the Infinite.

Love. Nor is this moral ideal without a sacred passion; at least to ordinary men; though it must be confessed that Spinoza, in the stillness of his sacred peace, ignored the word. But he still held that the larger our view of the Universe and of our communion therewith, the more we have of God in us and the more do we realize an "intellectual love" towards Him. That this in his case was no barren sentiment, but a genuine moral inspiration, was proved by his life; for truly "he endured as seeing Him who is invisible." And it was not by faculties wholly wanting to smaller men that he did this. For though his intellect was in some respects almost beyond compare, it was rather by his self-subordinating contemplation that he was kept at peace. Indeed, he knew far less of the extended universe than our men of science do, and his doctrines of mind and thought are, by indisputable authorities, regarded as imperfect. But imagining what God must be, could we have an adequate idea not only of His Being—which Spinoza thought he had—but

PANTHEISM

of His infinite attributes and their modes—which Spinoza recognized that he had not—he declared that love toward God was the very highest good. And it was supremely blessed in this, that it could engender no jealousy nor selfishness, nor sectarian zeal, but rather a large-hearted charity which would gather all mankind into the present heaven of that love.

AFTERWORD.

Spinoza's Apparent Failure. NOTWITHSTANDING the admiration, and even reverence, with which Spinoza was regarded by a few scholars during his life-time, it cannot be said that during the century following his death, in 1677, there was any wide acceptance of his ideas. The times were not favourable. For the political and social **Power of Ecclesiasticism.** power of ecclesiasticism, whether established, or unestablished, compelled men of science and philosophers to treat dominant creeds as consecrated ground, on which ordinary methods of research, reasoning or criticism could not be pursued. In saying this, I am far from accusing those illustrious men of insincerity. Some few of them, indeed, used a sort of cryptic satire to excuse to themselves an unwill-

PANTHEISM

Identification of Moral Interests with Conventional Beliefs. ing conformity. But, for the most part, the moral pressure of tradition and education compelled enlightened men to identify the doctrines of a personal God, Creation, Fall, Redemption and Immortality with moral interests vitally essential to human welfare. Under such circumstances a prudent conservatism was inevitable.

Gradual Spread of Spinoza's Influence. Yet, notwithstanding these restraining influences, the thoughts breathed forth by the lonely thinker were as living seed wafted abroad, and falling here and there on good ground, germinated and brought forth fruit. Sometimes his influence was acknowledged, sometimes it was repudiated; but it was there, nevertheless. It is doubtful

Fichte. whether Fichte's idealism could have taken the form it did had not Spinoza preceded him. Hegel, setting out on his great

Hegel. intellectual career with a resolve to defend the faith once delivered to the saints, yet traces its roots to a philosophy of Being which, at any rate, looks very like Pantheism. This is perhaps delicate ground to tread. For if one is asked whether one understands Hegel, one is

AFTERWORD

tempted to answer, like the pious Scotch lady when her friends enquired whether she had understood the minister's sermon, "Hech, sirs, d'ye think I'd presume?" Still, not my own reading of him only, but Mr. Haldane's profoundly interesting interpretations given in his *Gifford Lectures*, make the impression that Hegel's eternal process is always a projection of subject as object and redintegration of the two. And this goes on, not only on the infinite, but on the finite scale, amidst the infinite number of processes which constitute the Whole of Being. But this seems to leave no room for creation out of nothing, and it is to that extent pantheistic. There are doubtless saving interpretations, but it is difficult to follow them; and they cannot cancel the initial postulate of one eternal process, consisting in the relations of infinite subject, object and reunion. On such a system I do not see how there can be anything but God, and, therefore, notwithstanding his aversion to the name, count Hegel a Pantheist.

Goethe and Wordsworth. Goethe and Wordsworth, in many inspired passages of their poetry, echo the faith of Spinoza. Wordsworth, of course, in the reaction from his first expectations of the new order that he hoped to see arise out of the French Revolution, was inclined to magnify the importance of established religious ceremonies and creeds. But we cannot suppose that he ever repented of his reverence for Nature as a divine revelation. And we may believe that he continued to regard his practically pantheistic visions as an insight into the eternal reality from which the detailed schemes of orthodox theology were projected.

Schleiermacher. That Schleiermacher was much indebted to Spinoza is abundantly evident from his own words. He spoke of "the holy repudiated Spinoza." He declared that "the high world-spirit penetrated him; the Infinite was his beginning and his end; the universe his only and eternal love. In holy innocence and lowliness, he mirrored himself in the eternal world, and saw himself as its most love-worthy image. He was full of religion and of the Holy Spirit; and therefore he stands alone and unreachable, master in his art above the profane multitude, without disciples and without citizenship." [1]

[1] Quoted by Dr. J. Hunt, in his *Essay on Pantheism*, p. 312.

AFTERWORD

Anglican Broad Churchmen. Coming down to Anglican Broad Churchmen, it would scarcely be fair to quote isolated utterances as proofs of their Pantheism. And yet when Frederick Robertson asked, "What is this world itself but the form of Deity whereby the manifoldness and beauty of His mind manifests itself?" and still farther, when he quotes with approval Channing's word, that "perhaps matter is but a mode of thought," the most earnest Pantheist would hardly desire more. For the conception of the Universe involved must surely exclude the real being, or even the real existence, of anything but God. Matthew Arnold never committed himself to Pantheism, nor, indeed, to any other theory of the Universe. For his delicate humour and lambent satire always had in view simply the practical object of clearing a plain way for the good life through the "Aberglaube" of theology. His description of God as "the Power not ourselves which makes for righteousness," might seem, in fact, the negation of Pantheism, because, if God is not ourselves, there is something other than God. But the man who deliberately justified the loose phraseology of the Bible about infinite Being, by the plea that it was language "thrown out" at an object infinitely transcending linguistic expression, ought not himself to be pinned to the implications logically deducible from his own words "thrown out" at the same transcendant object. And, though Matthew Arnold was too literary to be a Pantheist, that is, though he thought more of forms of expression than of ultimate reality, his satirical disintegration of the creeds, wherever it is effective, makes Pantheism the only *religious* alternative. So-called "secular" and godless alternatives may be offered; but their incongruity with the whole evolution of humanity from prehistoric animism to the higher Pantheism will make their doom short and sure.

Why Pantheism as a Religion was called Modern. In the earlier part of this essay I made the remark that Pantheism as a religion is almost entirely modern. The context, however, clearly showed what was meant; for several pages have been occupied with indications of the ideas and teaching of individual Pantheists from Xenophanes to Spinoza. But we do not usually take much note of a religion that is confined to one or two men in an age. If it dies out we treat it merely as a curiosity, or an intellectual puzzle, like the dreams of Jacob Boehme, or the atheistic ecclesiasticism

AFTERWORD

of Comte. But, if it afterwards shows symptoms of unexpected adaptation to the mental and moral conditions of a newer world, and if, on account of this adaptation, it gains a hold on men who are neither philosophers nor metaphysicians, but only religious, it demands our consideration on far other grounds than those of intellectual curiosity.

Pantheistic Tendencies of Contemporary Thought. Now it has only been during the second half of the last century that Pantheism has been able to claim attention as a religion in such a sense as this. As to the fact there can hardly be any dispute. For not only has it become ever a more prominent motive in the music of the poets, and not only are all rationalizations of Christianity more or less transparent disguises of Pantheism, but I may safely appeal to those ordinary members of intelligent society who are neither poets, nor divines, nor philosophers, whether the freest and most confidential interchange of religious thought does not continually verge on a faith which merges everything in God.

Caused by the Mutual Pressure of Science and Faith. Nor are the reasons of this tendency far to seek. Indeed, they are palpable and conspicuous in the mutual pressure of science and faith. For, on the one

PANTHEISM

hand science has made unthinkable the old-world conception of a three-storeyed Universe, constructed by an artificer God, who suddenly awoke from an eternity of idleness to make Heaven, Earth, and Hell—a conception involving a King of kings, enthroned like an eastern monarch, and sending forth His ministering spirits, or appointing His angel deputies to direct and govern at His beck. Or if it be said that never, except in the ages of primeval simplicity, or amongst later generations living under primeval conditions, has such a conception been entertained, it would be difficult for the "broadest" Churchman to say what has been put in its place. It is vain to remind us how later Christianity has patronised

The Nebular Hypothesis taken alone involves Absurdity. nebular hypotheses and the doctrine of evolution. For these give no definite substitute whatever for the old story, that Elohim "spoke, and it was done—he commanded, and it stood fast." Whence the fiery mists by the rotation and cooling of which the worlds were slowly evolved? We are told that the same process is going on now within the ken of astronomers. But does any one suppose that in those realms of space God is evoking something out of nothing, or saying "be," and "there

AFTERWORD

is"? No; we are assured that these fiery mists are formed by the collision of misguided orbs; and we are even asked—or, at least we *were* asked—to believe that this process must go on until all systems are agglomerated in one orb, to be ultimately congealed into stone. What, then, is the office of the Creator according to this scheme, as repulsive as it is absurd? It would appear that, at some moment in a vacuous eternity, He calls matter out of nothing, whirls it into fiery vortices, and then lets it cool down to the absolute zero wherein death reigns for ever.

The Protest of Faith. But, after all, "there is a spirit in man," and "the inspiration of the Almighty," of the Eternal, of the glorious Whole to which we belong, stirs in us a protest against this blasphemy of ignorance. Ignorance, I say, for it was not the knowledge of our wise men that whispered such things, but their sense of the vacuity beyond their knowledge. Up to certain bounds, their grasp of facts, their insight into physical order, their mathematical skill, were beyond all praise. But beyond that bound, aye, and within it, in every inconceivable mode of the action of force, as, for example, in gravitation, brooded the Unknowable. And it was not their

PANTHEISM

Sustained by Latest Science. knowledge, but their ignorance that entailed absurd issues. Already there are signs that even celestial physics and mathematics will refuse to endorse as final so revolting a scheme of material evolution and devolution, ending only in universal death.[1] And when once the re-birth of new order out of the old is seen to be everywhere and eternally taking place, then all the hints given us by science of the ultimate oneness of all things, converge in the faith that All is God, and God is All. For certainly, the latest observations on Matter suggest that all forms of it are variations of one ultimate Substance. And the **Which Suggests an Infinite Unity.** convertibility of forces, as well as the conservation of force, point to one eternal energy. Nor is the duality thus suggested any final conclusion. For few, I imagine, would now contend that, in the last result Matter and Force are fundamentally different things. In fact, Monism holds the field; and though the evolution of human opinion is very slow, it appears safe to predict that the triumph of that world theory is assured.

[1] See *The Religion of the Universe*, pp. 128-30.

AFTERWORD

Idea of Creation Incongruous with Modern Knowledge. This result is additionally secured by the increasing incongruity felt between the immeasurable vastness of the Universe, even as known, and the idea of creation out of nothing. When the Almighty could be seriously pictured as constructing chambers for Himself and His heavenly host above, the middle floor of earth for the children of men, and the abyss for ghosts and devils, the notion that His word evoked that puny structure from nothing might be invested by poets and prophets with a certain grandeur. Each part of the work had an object as conceivable as that of each floor in a house; and, according to petty human notions of utility, nothing was wasted. But now, when our astronomers confront us with countless millions of orbs, to whose extension in space no bound can be proved, while some of them tell us that the whole immensity is a desert of alternate fire and darkness, with no spark of finite intellect except in our tiny earth, some of us, at least, cannot help feeling that the notion of a personal divine worker calling this huge enigma out of blank eternal nothing, is enormously and utterly incongruous both with reverence and common sense.

PANTHEISM

And if the Pantheist in these days be asked, "What interpretation then do you propose?" his answer is, "I propose none. I take things as they are. In their totality they are unknowable, as, indeed, even science finds they are in their infinitesimal parts." But we need not on this account lose "the divinity that shapes our ends."

Pantheistic Morality. For, between the infinite and the infinitesimal the human experience realizes itself in surroundings which, when observed and reflected on, make the impression of ordered relations of parts. By a necessity of our finite and individual existence as centres of action—a necessity of which we can give no account—we present those relations to ourselves in forms of time and space. Then, when our experience is large enough and ripe enough, being enriched and stimulated by the stored-up experience of humanity, as recorded in tradition, custom, Bibles, and Epics, we attain to the moral sense, and realize that we

The Law of the Whole. are bound to be loyal to something greater than self. That "greater" may be the tribe, the nation, humanity or God. But in far the larger number of cases in which this sense of willing loyalty is aroused, its cause is the appeal to us of some whole of which

AFTERWORD

we form a part. Certainly this is so with the patriot and the philanthropist. Indeed, it would be difficult, or impossible, to find any human relationship, from the family upwards, through the wider circles of school, club, municipality, nationality, in which this sense of loyalty or devotion to the law of the whole is not the best incentive to devotion.

Yet, when we come to contemplate the final and supreme object of devotion, the Eternal Himself, it has been almost the universal custom to make a surprising exception, and to regard religion as maintainable only by recognition of a tremendous outward authority, to which only such loyalty is possible as in barbarous times was fostered towards a personal chieftain, or feudal king. Now Pantheism holds this to be an error,

Of that Law of the Whole Loyalty to God in the Supreme Application. and regards obedience and devotion to God as the ultimate and most inspiring application of that principle of the loyalty of the part to the whole which runs through all morality.

Conclusion. Why should we be supposed to be without God because we acknowledge Him to be superpersonal, and " past finding out " ? Or why should we be suspected of denying the

PANTHEISM

divinity of evolution because we do not believe the Eternal All to be subject to it ? This instinct of loyalty, in the sense of self-subordination to any greater Whole of which we are part, the distinction of right and wrong thence arising, and the aspiration after a moral ideal, are not of man's invention. Speaking, as we cannot help doing, in terms of time, I hold that the germs of this higher creature-life were always in the divine unity out of which man is evolved. And in pursuing the inspirations of that higher life, as experience suggests them, humanity has always had a guide and a saviour in the Living God, of whom the race life-time of man is an infinitesimal phase. In such an interpretation of man's relations to God there is nothing necessarily hostile to any form of genuine religion.[1] True, there are in the creeds many statements which we cannot accept in the letter. But there are few which have not some spiritual suggestion for us. And if we can attain to that intellectual love of God in which Spinoza was absorbed, we have no quarrel with any mode of sincere devotion. Pious Catholic,

[1] Limitations of space must be my apology for reference to an enlargement of this topic in " A Pantheistic Sermon " at the end of *The Religion of the Universe*.

AFTERWORD

Protestant, Vedantist, Mohammedan—all, by the implicit, though unrecognised necessities of their faith, worship the same God as ourselves. But the wrangles of sectarian zeal no longer concern us : for we have passed

"To where beyond these voices there is peace."

Chronological Syllabus

Relation of Pantheism to Religious Evolution

Primæval Period.

Admittedly conjectural, but almost necessarily assumed. When man first emerged, he must have been like the baby described by Tennyson, and mixed himself with the world. In fact it was a *pre-animistic stage*. Life was everywhere, but it had not taken the form of ghosts or portents.

Fetishism, Animism.

Prehistoric; former, the notion of souls able to detach themselves from bodies, and therefore to survive death (ancestor worship); latter, a fascination by strange-looking, weird, or imposing objects enshrining some sacred potency for good or evil, mostly the latter; both survive all over the world in various modified forms; and are traceable even in the doctrines and ritual of advanced theological and ceremonial religions.

Polytheism.

The belief in many personal gods, among whom, however, one may be a " primus inter pares " ; a higher development of Animism ; prevalent in Europe down to the fourth and even fifth century A.D., and in India down to the present time.

Henotheism.

The local or national worship of one god to the neglect of others, while the existence and local power of the gods of other tribes is not denied. This seems to have been the religion of Israel from the beginning of the kingdom as distinguished from the loose federation of tribes, until the time of the Deuteronomist, i.e. according to Carpenter and Battersby and the general tendency of recent authoritative opinion, some time in the seventh century B.C. Henotheism was also favoured by local populations in ancient Egypt.

Monotheism.

The worship of one personal God as the only deity, all others being treated either as devils or as "nothing in the world" (1 Cor. viii. 4; x. 20). This began to be the religion of Israel about the time of the Deuteronomist, and was much promoted by the greater prophets, the Isaiahs, Jeremiah and Ezekiel. But it does not appear to have been quite definitely and finally established until after the captivity and the consecration of the Second Temple. The Monotheism of Mahommed owed a good deal to Jewish tradition; but it was and is even more intensely "unitarian" than the religion of Israel. Under Christianity the doctrines of the Trinity and the Incarnation have prepared the way for a larger conception of Deity and a wider tolerance.

Pantheism.

The idea of the Universe as one living Being, of which all creatures and things are "parts and proportions," and therefore in themselves nothing. This religion of the Universe was really implicit in Fetishism and Animism, much as a tree is implicit in the seed. In that sense it is prehistoric and almost coeval with the first emergence of man. But perhaps the first conscious and express realization of what was implicit in Animism is to be found in the Vedic literature, where all gods and men and animals and things are regarded as modifications of Brahmā's being. The successive steps in the development of Pantheism, parallel with or under the guise of more partial religions, are traced in the preceding pages.

Epochs in the Progress toward Pantheism.

The Upanishads—From about 1000 B.C. and onward, p. 27 ante.

Xenophanes of Elea—570 to 480 B.C., p. 39.

Philo of Alexandria—Contemporary with Christ, p. 48.

Bhagavad Gîtâ—Date disputed, but certainly after the Christian era, p. 29.

Appearance of the Fourth Gospel (called St. John's)—About 125 A.D.

Neoplatonism—Early Christian centuries, p. 50.

The Mystics—Middle Ages, p. 54

Spinoza—1632–1677 A.D., p. 56, etc.

Selected Works bearing on Pantheism.

Essay on Pantheism, by the Rev. JOHN HUNT, D.D. Isbister & Co. 1884.

Sacred Books of the East, translated by various Oriental Scholars and edited by F. MAX MÜLLER. (Especially Vol. I.) Clarendon Press.

The Bhagavad Gîtâ, translated by JOHN DAVIES, M.A. Kegan Paul & Co. 1893.

Spinoza, His Life and Philosophy, by Sir FREDERICK POLLOCK, Bart. Second edition. Duckworth & Co. 1899.

Ethic of Benedict de Spinoza, translated by W. HALE WHITE and AMELIA H. STIRLING. Third edition. Duckworth & Co. 1899.

Christian Pantheism (in "The Mystery of Matter"), by J. ALLANSON PICTON. Macmillan & Co. 1873.

The Religion of the Universe, by J. ALLANSON PICTON. Macmillan & Co. 1904.

Ethisch Pantheisme, by P. H. HUGENHOLZ, junr. Amsterdam, Van Holkema en Warendorf. 1903. (Not translated).

Butler & Tanner, The Selwood Printing Works, Frome, and London.

RETURN TO the circulation desk of any
University of California Library
or to the
NORTHERN REGIONAL LIBRARY FACILITY
Bldg. 400, Richmond Field Station
University of California
Richmond, CA 94804-4698

ALL BOOKS MAY BE RECALLED AFTER 7 DAYS
- 2-month loans may be renewed by calling (510) 642-6753
- 1-year loans may be recharged by bringing books to NRLF
- Renewals and recharges may be made 4 days prior to due date.

DUE AS STAMPED BELOW

MAY 2 0 2002

12,000 (11/95)

Ingram Content Group UK Ltd.
Milton Keynes UK
UKHW020953130623
423332UK00005B/190